CENTRAL SMT BUSES

DAVID DEVOY

First published 2016

Amberley Publishing
The Hill, Stroud
Gloucestershire, GL5 4EP

www.amberley-books.com

Copyright © David Devoy, 2016

The right of David Devoy to be identified as the Author of this work has been asserted in accordance with the Copyrights, Designs and Patents Act 1988.

ISBN 978 1 4456 5480 5 (print)
ISBN 978 1 4456 5481 2 (ebook)

All rights reserved. No part of this book may be reprinted or reproduced or utilised in any form or by any electronic, mechanical or other means, now known or hereafter invented, including photocopying and recording, or in any information storage or retrieval system, without the permission in writing from the Publishers.

British Library Cataloguing in Publication Data.
A catalogue record for this book is available from the British Library.

Typesetting by Amberley Publishing.
Printed in the UK.

A Brief History of Central SMT

The late Robert Grieves left us all a wonderful gift in his book *Central SMT: The First 40 Years*. Robert took the story to the early 1970s, and sadly because he is no longer with us, it falls to me to try and finish the story. I dedicate this book to Robert and thank him for the wonderful body of work he left behind. Hopefully I can add a little bit more to the story. Thanks to my good friend Alistair Scobbie for helping me with a few pictures from his collection.

The origins of the company began in 1926 when the Glasgow General Omnibus Company began operations around Hamilton. The firm was closely linked with London General and originally used the same livery of red and cream. They operated out of Clydesdale Garage located in Bothwell Road in Hamilton; use of the depot was continued by Central SMT until 1988. Right from the start the firm began an aggressive takeover of many of their competitors, and road haulage was added to the portfolio. Expansion had been too quick and the firm was forced to sell a stake in the business to SMT of Edinburgh in 1928. The company had started operating services along the north bank of the River Clyde into Dunbartonshire, and built Waterloo Street bus station in Glasgow. As time went on SMT built up their stake in the company and chairman William Thomson changed the livery to SMT blue in 1932 after taking full control. It was his intention that all SMT-owned companies would share a common colour scheme of blue.

John Torrance was an electrical engineer who began operating buses in 1926 under the title of J. W. & R. Torrance, which were also based in Hamilton. They built a new depot at Burnbank Road, which continued to be used by Central SMT until 1966. The Torrance Company, although seen as a large operator, joined the Lanarkshire Bus Owners Association (A1 Service) for a period, before competing with their former allies. This successful firm was taken over by the Glasgow General Omnibus Company in 1932, and GOC was renamed as Central SMT later in the year.

Another major player in the area was Stewart and McDonald. In a period of overexpansion they found they could not pay their fuel bill to a local filling station owned by Robert Dick. Robert accepted a share of the business as payment and took over the running of the firm. The livery used was dark red and brown, which Robert

Dick insisted be kept after the firm became owned by the SMT Group. Robert was appointed as the first general manager of Central SMT and responsible for merging all the former fleets into one cohesive unit. He successfully argued his corner that Central SMT be allowed to keep its own livery and identity, helped by John Sword of the newly created Western SMT who was also adamant that the same would apply to Western.

In among all the bus activity, much of the area was covered by the trams of the Hamilton, Motherwell and Wishaw Tramways Company which was owned by the British-Thomson Houston Company based in Rugby. The trams began in 1903 and used a livery of blue and white. The company was renamed as the Lanarkshire Traction Company in August 1903 under the management of Gustavus Frederick Moller. Gustavus was sure the future lay in operating buses instead of trams, and obtained powers to run buses up to five miles beyond any of the firms tram tracks. The early buses proved unsuccessful and were discontinued. Four years later Gustavus began operating his own buses before offering his company to his employer, with a threat that he would expand the business if they refused. By the 1920s the company had to greatly increase their bus fleet as other companies creamed off many passengers. The livery was changed to green. The general strike of 1926 led to a huge fall-off in passenger numbers, lasting a couple of years before recovering, although a major depot fire put the company in dire straits. Control of the company passed to Daimler in 1930, and the trams were abandoned the following year. An offer from the SMT Group was accepted in 1932. The Central SMT management took over and changed the livery to that of Central SMT, but the company retained its own identity and fleet name, often running jointly with Central. The company was merged with Central SMT in 1949 after the SMT Group became state-owned. Gustavus Moller resigned in 1926 to set up his own company under the title of Lowland Motorways and was based in Glasgow, and eventually sold the business to SMT for a very large undisclosed sum in 1958. The SMT Group was eventually renamed as the Scottish Transport Group.

Central SMT went from strength to strength becoming the most profitable company in the state-owned sector, often making as much as the rest of the Scottish Bus Group put together. A number of double-deckers joined the fleet and very close headways were operated throughout industrial Lanarkshire. Depots were maintained at Motherwell, Hamilton, Wishaw, East Kilbride, Harthill, Old Kilpatrick and Carluke with a couple of outstations as well. Livery was dark red and cream, with coaches using two-tone blue from 1955 until 1977. A major acquisition was the Hamilton firm of Laurie Bros t/a Chieftain of Hamilton. This added thirty-one vehicles, but more importantly allowed greater access to the new town of East Kilbride.

As the years progressed much of the heavy industry closed down leading to cuts in bus services as unemployment rose. Depots were closed as the fleet shrunk and cost savings were introduced where possible. The fleet name became Central Scottish from 1978. In 1985 the Scottish Bus Group decided to reorganise their subsidiary companies to prepare for deregulation of bus services and match operating areas to local council boundaries. In Central's case this meant that the operations on the North bank of the Clyde passed to the newly created Kelvin Scottish, but the Eastern Scottish operations based on Airdrie were added. Central became the biggest company in the Bus Group with a fleet of 470 vehicles. In December 1988 management of the company passed to Kelvin Scottish and by January 1989 the drivers, cleaners and shunters went on strike due to proposed changes to their working conditions. The strike was costing the company £400,000 a week, but more significantly other operators were tempted to start up their own services in the area. The strike ended on 24 February after seven weeks and lost the company £3 million. Drastic action had to be taken and the entire Harrier network in Glasgow was abandoned with sixty-five drivers losing their jobs. The brand was now seen as toxic and plans were made to paint the fleet in EK Chieftain, Lanarkshire Bus and Monklands Bus liveries. It was also announced that the company would be fully merged with Kelvin Scottish to form Kelvin Central Buses from 22 May.

Staff again withdrew their labour only six weeks after the return to work following a disagreement over the sacking of the shop stewards after they had called a staff meeting to discuss new rosters that led to a disruption of services. Negotiations with ACAS failed and management warned that if the strike was not called off the company would be closed down. Dismissal notices were prepared for staff that refused to come back to work. Only ten drivers out of 600 turned up for work on 8 May. The strike finally ended on 31 May. Huge fleet and service reductions followed, and the fleet finally merged with Kelvin Central Buses on 17 July 1989. East Kilbride and Wishaw depots were closed with 180 jobs lost. The combined company now faced more competition than they could ever have imagined. The fight back would soon begin, and the story will continue in the next book, Kelvin Central Buses.

GM 8823 was a Leyland Titan PD2/30/Alexander L31/28R purchased new by Central SMT as their fleet number L583 in October 1957, and would run for the company until 1972. There were three services from Balloch (132/133/136), and the journey to Glasgow via the West End, Clydebank and Old Kilpatrick lasted around 1 hour 12 minutes.

LHS 736V was a front-engined Volvo Ailsa B55-10 fitted with Alexander AV-type H44/35F bodywork delivered new in October 1979 as AH12. The H in the fleet number indicated that it was built to full height, and could not be used on services from East Kilbride to Glasgow via Busby due to a railway bridge height restriction.

Central launched their 'Harrier' minibuses in 1986, with seventeen of these Dodge S56/Alexander B21F. R11 (D311 MHS) was captured in Glasgow on service M2, which ran to Rutherglen via Spittal. A further batch was delivered the following year, which took the numbers up to thirty-one, but heavy competition from Strathclyde Buses forced their redeployment elsewhere.

Scottish Citylink Coaches was formed in June 1985 during the reorganisation of the Scottish Bus Group to coordinate the long-distance express services operated by the various subsidiaries, and overnight became the largest operator of long-distance express services within Scotland and from Scotland to England. They hired in coaches as required and Central provided DD13 (A204 UYS) in Citylink livery. This Dennis Dorchester was bodied by Alexander to their TC design and seated forty-seven passengers.

For many years East Kilbride had no actual bus station, and services loaded up in Churchill Avenue. T22 (AGM 622B) was bound for Nerston on service 77. This Leyland Leopard/Alexander Y type had been new in 1964, but didn't enter service until January 1965. It was converted to OMO in 1971, and would see further service with Marbill of Beith and Millport Motors after disposal in 1981.

LC2 (B102 BYS) was a Leyland Cub CU435/Duple Dominant B33F purchased new in May 1985, and was caught in East Kilbride working on service 128 which connected the town centre and West Mains. The Leyland Cub CU series was manufactured by Leyland between 1979 and 1987, but sales were disappointing.

N29 (MDS 862V) was a Leyland National NL116L11/1R B52F delivered new in April 1980, later swapped with sister company Kelvin Scottish, and passed to Kelvin Central Buses in 1989. It was then rebuilt to National Greenway specification by East Lancs Coachbuilders in May 1994, but remained a one-off with KCB. The building in the background was Lewis's, which was a chain of British department stores that operated from 1856 to 1991, when the company went into administration.

GSU 842T was a Leyland Leopard PSU3C/3R/Alexander Y-type B53F new as T360 in April 1979, shown posed at the company's Motherwell Depot. The Leopard would become Central's chosen bus with a total 440 serving in the fleet over the years, mostly built to the short-window design. The company was very slow to adopt semi-automatic transmission and continued to specify narrow entrance doors.

In June 1985 the Scottish Bus Group reorganised their subsidiary companies. In Central's case this meant it lost Old Kilpatrick depot to Kelvin Scottish and acquired Clarkston depot from Eastern Scottish. SP3 (CSG 791S) came with the services around Airdrie and was of an unfamiliar type to Central. It was a Seddon Pennine VII/Plaxton Supreme C45F, new as Eastern Scottish YS791 in April 1978.

EGB 77T was the prototype Dennis Dominator for the Scottish Bus Group, and was delivered as Central Scottish D1 in October 1978. It went on loan to Midland at Milngavie depot for comparison tests with an Ailsa, a Metrobus, an Olympian and a Leyland Fleetline. Ironically the Fleetline came out on top even though the model was being discontinued, and in view of Central's dissatisfaction with the type. A fleet of fifty-one Dominators was built up for use on the busy services to Glasgow.

Central purchased fifteen Leyland Leopard/Alexander T-type coaches for use on private hires and longer services. T393 (PGA 833V) was new in July 1980 and carries the zigzag livery style adopted in later years. The Redline name applied referred to a network of commuter journeys that the company built up after deregulation.

The Bristol Lodekka was a low-height double-decker bus built by Bristol Commercial Vehicles in England. It was the first production bus design to have no step up from the entrance throughout the lower deck, and the company manufactured over 5,200 of them from 1949 to 1968. It was only available to the UK state-owned bus sector, and B188 (AGM 688B) was awaiting collection from the Eastern Coachworks factory in Lowestoft in May 1964.

The use of broadside adverts was a fashion in the early 1980s, and Central AH4 (BGG 254S) demonstrates the point with a scheme for Drybroughs Burns Heavy. This Edinburgh-based brewer was later purchased by Allied-Lyons and closed down. The Ailsa order was originally placed by Fife Scottish, but redistributed between Eastern, Western and Central Scottish.

Central SMT had a strained relationship with Hutchison's of Overtown in the 1960s when the independent expanded their services in the Wishaw and Motherwell areas. At the time Central was suffering from staff shortages and was not in a position to launch new routes. After appeals and counter appeals Barbara Castle, the Minister for Transport, ordered that the two firms had to coordinate their services. The result was that the SBG purchased a stake in Hutchison's with an option to purchase the company in the future.

Central purchased fifty Dennis Dominators fitted with Alexander's stylish R-type bodywork. D46 (MNS 46Y) carries promotional material for the SBG 'Best Bus' campaign as it heads to Duntocher. Routes were linked up to form long cross-city services across Glasgow that cut down on vehicles cluttering up the city centre.

LT7 (MNS 7Y) was a Leyland Tiger TRBTL11/2R/Alexander TE-type C49F delivered new in March 1983. The livery used on these vehicles was a huge step forward for such a conservative company. LT7 was working for Scottish Citylink on service 500 bound for Gourock. MNS 7Y would later join Fife Scottish for further service.

NGM 167G was a Bristol VRT/ECW H43/34F purchased new by Central SMT as their fleet number BN367 in November 1969. Central had a batch of 20 VRTs with transverse engines, similar to the Daimler Fleetline. They were no more successful and were swapped with the National Bus Company on a one-for-one basis for half-cab Lodekkas in 1973. This time it was all the VRT operators in the Scottish Bus Group who were involved, but ironically many of these discarded buses had very long lives south of the border.

The pits at the former Eastern Scottish depot at Clarkston plays host to two Seddon Pennine VII/Alexander T-type C49F inherited with the garage. SP13 retains Eastern Scottish livery, while SP15 has already been repainted by Central. Thirty-three Seddons were added to the fleet with the Airdrie operations, and they were quite a mixed bunch with bus and coach examples bodied with both Alexander Y- and T-type bodywork and Plaxton Supreme coachwork.

When Scottish Citylink launched a service connecting Edinburgh with Paisley via East Kilbride it was left to Central to provide the vehicles. A pair of TE-type Leyland Tigers were the usual performers. MNS 10Y was captured in Paisley Gilmour Street working on a return journey to the Scottish capital wearing full Citylink livery.

MHS 19P was a Leyland Leopard PSU3C/3R/Alexander Y-type B53F bought new in March 1976 as T241, and based at Gavinburn Depot. Central specified straight mouldings on the waistband of these buses and produced a clean modern effect. The garage passed to Kelvin Scottish in June 1985 and was closed by Kelvin Central Buses in May 1996.

Fourteen Leyland National 2s were added to the fleet in June 1985 when Clarkston depot was acquired. N55 was an NL116L11/1R B52F model new as Eastern Scottish N579 in April 1980. Its stay with Central was brief however, as it passed to Kelvin Scottish the following year as their 1219. It moved on to Western Scottish in 1988 and lasted into Stagecoach days.

VTY 131Y was a Leyland Tiger TRCTL11/3R/Plaxton Paramount 3200 C49Ft first registered by Northern General in June 1983, but I believe it was only on loan from Leyland Bus. It returned to Leyland and was purchased by Central Scottish in 1984, but as a fifty-three seater and numbered as C1. It later gained Scottish Citylink livery and was transferred to Kelvin, later becoming WLT 388.

In 1970 Leyland announced it was to cease making the Leopard PSU3/3R, which had a manual gearbox and O600 engine. All production was to be of models with the larger O680 engine and Pneumocyclic semi-automatic gearbox. Scottish Bus Group were by this time the only purchaser of the old variant and stated they would not buy semi-automatic Leopards, regarding the O680 as too thirsty. They persuaded Seddon to build a chassis with a Gardner engine and manual gearbox, of which JFS 977X was an example.

Central purchased the business of Laurie Bros t/a Chieftain of Hamilton in 1961 and added thirty-one assorted buses to the fleet. Sixteen were ex-London Park Royal bodied Leyland RTLs, including HL201 (KGU 433). The Scottish Bus Group paid a fortune for the Chieftain business primarily to get control of East Kilbride which would be expanded as a new town. The Chieftain livery would be resurrected in a last ditch attempt to save the company in its final days.

Central's final order for new double-deckers in 1986 saw the Leyland Olympian chosen with dual-purpose Alexander bodywork. The batch of ten operated from East Kilbride on Redline commuter express services to Glasgow. They wore this attractive variation of the livery, featuring the Redline fleet name. LO7 (C807 KHS) looks smart as it arrives in Glasgow.

T255 (MHS 33P) was a Leyland Leopard PSU3C/3R/Alexander B53F delivered new in March 1976. It was working in Glasgow city centre, a most unsuitable vehicle for busy city work with high steps, manual gearbox and narrow doorway. It would become Kelvin Central 1415, and ultimately be a driver training vehicle with KCB and First Midland Red.

One aspect of the introduction of corporate fleet names by the Scottish Bus Group in 1978 was the tidying up of Central's double-deck livery. BL316 (FGM 316D) shows the effect nicely. This Bristol Lodekka FLF6G/ECW H44/32F was new in May 1966 and still looked smart. On disposal it would pass to Stewart's of Dalmuir for further service.

Central's dissatisfaction with the Daimler Fleetline led to a swap with other SBG companies. Eastern Scottish transferred a batch of Leyland Leopards in return, including T283 (PFS 562M) seen in Motherwell. These buses differed in having a 'flash' in the livery at waist level and stood out from the indigenous examples.

Wolverhampton-based manufacturer Guy Motors had developed an underfloor-engined version of their Arab chassis, the UF, which was coupled with Alexander Coronation bodywork in March 1952. Central purchased a batch of ten coaches that featured a central entrance, and they were allocated fleet numbers K35–44. The first of the batch was K35 (GVD 35) which lasted until 1964.

T9 (AGM 609B) was an Alexander B53F bodied Leyland Leopard PSU3/1R delivered new in 1964. The batch started with fleet number T7 following on from six short Leopards purchased in 1961 which were originally numbered T1–6, but later TS1–6 to differentiate them. T9 ran until March 1976 when it was sold to W Alexander & Sons (Northern) as their NPE40.

Central ran a small fleet of midi-buses on local services in East Kilbride, which used roads that were often unsuitable for normal buses and had a 7-foot-6-inch-wide restriction applied. 845 HUS was a Bedford VAS1/Duple (Northern) B29F that had started life with MacBrayne's of Glasgow in June 1963, although was acquired from Highland Omnibuses in September 1973.

There is nothing like the sight of a brand new bus and B248 BYS was a Leyland Tiger TRBLXB/2RH/Alexander TS-type B53F new to Central Scottish as LT48 in April 1985. It later became Kelvin Central Buses 1248, and later First Glasgow ST368. This was East Kilbride Garage which was opened in 1956 in Nerston Industrial Estate, and closed in 1990 under Kelvin Central ownership.

D10 (TYS 263W) was a Dennis Dominator DD137B/Alexander RL-type H45/34F purchased new in June 1981. It was bound for Faifley after routes were linked to form cross-city connections, making the wording of the Clydesdale Bank broadside advert quite appropriate.

T183 (AGM 683L) was snapped during the Scottish Bus Group's 'Best Bus Around' campaign, which all subsidiaries had a version of. T183 was screened up to work a peak-hour express journey on service X1 from Glasgow to East Kilbride, and was a standard manual synchromesh gearbox Leyland Leopard which the company bought up until 1979.

LT11 (OUS 11Y) was a Leyland Tiger TRBTL11/2R/Alexander TS-type B53F purchased new in July 1983. The TS was specially developed for Central as the company didn't like Alexander's P type then in production, so Alexander's built a basic version TE type instead. The livery used, although attractive, was not practical for service buses as any replacement panels often had two or three colour breaks on them.

T152 (XGM 452L) was a Leyland Leopard PSU3/3R/Alexander B53F delivered new in September 1972. This view taken in Luss shows the pre-corporate style of fleet names carried before 1978. On disposal this bus would pass to Silver Service of Darnley Dale for further service.

The Anderston Centre was a mixed-use commercial and residential complex, with the bus station underneath located in Glasgow and completed in 1972 as one of the earliest examples of the megastructure style of urban renewal schemes, fashionable in the 1960s. Central shared the station with Western, but it was quickly seen as a rundown part of the city. B211 (AGM 711B) was a 1964 Bristol Lodekka/ECW H33/27RD caught as it emerged from the gloom.

MSJ 385P was a Seddon Pennine VII/Alexander T-type C49F new as Western SMT S2579 in July 1976. It was converted for wheelchair use as C24DL and sold to Central in 1984 and initially allocated to Traction House, a location also known as Airbles depot. This was the last depot to be built for Central and was completed in 1962, adjacent to Traction House in Motherwell.

KGM 653F was a Leyland Leopard PSU3/1R/Alexander Y-type B53F new to Central as T53 in May 1968. It remained in use until stripped for spares in 1982. It was bound for Stathaven on service 54. With fifty-three seats, a standee Leopard had almost as many seats as an early, post-war double-decker, and they quickly became the standard Central SMT bus. By 1983 some 400 Leopards had been purchased new, as well as a number of second-hand examples from within the SBG.

DSC 976W was a Seddon Pennine VII/Plaxton Supreme Express C49F new to Eastern Scottish as their number YS976 in July 1981. It joined Central as SP32 in June 1985 with Clarkston depot and was passing through Airdrie complete with 'Best Bus Around' lettering. The Bus Group had the first example of the Pennine VII bodied and delivered in October 1973 and the last entered service after a run of 527 chassis in 1982.

RHN 945F was one of the buses involved in the NBC-SBG vehicle swap. It was a Bristol Lodekka FLF6/ECW H38/32F purchased new by United Automobile as their L245 in February 1968, and passed to Northern General as number 2862. It became Central BE372 in 1973 and was leaving Glasgow Anderston bus station for Lanark. It featured the Cave-Brown-Cave heating system developed by a Professor of Engineering at Southampton University. He contested that it should be possible to deliver more heat with a greater airflow than would appear possible via a conventional fan-drive system as used on buses and coaches.

Central's first Leyland Nationals arrived in 1978 and were put to work on Hamilton town services. A batch of twenty Leopard chassis was changed for twenty Nationals, including N14 (EGB 91T) which entered service in January 1979. It passed to Kelvin Central in 1989, and quickly moved to Western Scottish. On disposal it joined the Birmingham Coach Company and later Lothian Buses.

The Dennis Dorchester was a mid-engined heavy-duty single-deck bus chassis manufactured by Dennis in small numbers between 1983 and 1988. About two thirds of the total number built were bought by Scottish Bus Group subsidiaries Western Scottish, Central Scottish and Clydeside Scottish. These consisted of twenty-three with Plaxton Paramount coach bodywork, and twenty-one with Alexander bodywork, with each of the three T-type variants represented – five each of the TS service bus and TE express semi-coach, and eleven of the TC full coach. DD3 (A103 RGE) was a TS example captured at Wishaw Cross.

St Andrews Square bus station opened in April 1957 with sixteen stances over five platforms, with underground subways connecting the platforms. By the late 1960s an office block was built on the air space above the station, but the building supports ate into the platforms thus reducing the space. The station closed on 2 July 2000 as part of developments of the site, which included a new bus station and Scotland's first Harvey Nichols store. Central Tiger LT9 (MNS 9Y) had just arrived on Scottish Citylink service X12.

BE240 (CGM 740C) is sitting at the Common Green stance in Strathaven screened up for a return trip to Glasgow. This Bristol Lodekka FLF6G/ECW H38/30F had been purchased new in May 1965. To protect private industry, state-owned bus manufacture was limited to set amounts each year and had to be negotiated with the government. Every now and then sanctions were given to build a certain amount of buses. As supply was limited this allowed the Bus Group to buy from other manufacturers.

Central's first two-tone blue Bedford/Duple coaches arrived in 1955, and this combination was to endure until 1977. The fleet was to span several variants of both chassis and bodies, but although intended for private hire work it was not uncommon to see them working on the lengthy 242/3/4 Limited Stop services between Glasgow and Biggar or Peebles. C45 (WGM 45K) was a Bedford YRQ/Duple Viceroy C45F bought new in March 1972 and caught in Peebles.

The Leyland Leopard was introduced in 1959, and developed from the Leyland Tiger Cub. One of the most important changes was the introduction of the more powerful o.600 engine and later-built chassis were fitted with the 11.1 litre o.680 engine. T434 (LUS 434Y) was a PSU3G/4R model fitted with Alexander Y-type B53F bodywork from the last batch supplied in January 1983.

The Leopard was also chosen for the coach fleet when more powerful vehicles were required. T370 (GSU 852T) was departing from the now closed Coliseum coach station in Blackpool with holidaymakers from Airdrie. T370 carried Alexander T-type C49F bodywork, was new in April 1979 and had a 4-speed ZF manual gearbox. It later worked for KCB, McColl's Coaches and Gibson's of Moffat.

T77 (OGM 277H) was an Alexander B53F bodied Leopard PSU3/1R bought new in 1970. It was leaving Buchanan bus station in Glasgow, which was built in 1977 and is the biggest bus station in Scotland with around 1,700 bus journeys departing every day, and over 40,000 passengers using these journeys on a daily basis.

C349 LVV was a Volvo B10M-61 Caetano Algarve C57F purchased new by Newton's of Dingwall in September 1985. Three months later it passed to the Scottish Bus Group with the business and was allocated to the Central Scottish fleet as their C9. It received Scottish Citylink livery and was working a 376 service when snapped in Cambridge. It passed to the merged KCB in 1989 and on disposal went to Marbill of Beith.

Central SMT received its first Leyland Leopards in 1961 when six short L2 models fitted with Alexander C41F bodywork arrived. They originally carried fleet numbers T1–6, but this was later changed to TS1–6 in order to differentiate between the later longer deliveries. TS4 (CGM 414) shows the design to good effect.

B104 (BGM 104) was a Bristol Lodekka LD6G/ECW H33/27R purchased new by Central SMT in March 1960. It was receiving mechanical attention at Gavinburn Depot which was built over the site of an ancient Roman fort. The garage and services passed to Kelvin Scottish in June 1985, later becoming Kelvin Central in 1989 and was finally closed in May 1996.

Motherwell was noted as the steel production capital of Scotland and sometimes nicknamed Steelopolis. Its skyline was dominated by the gasholder and three cooling towers of the Ravenscraig steel plant which closed in 1992. Central T130 (UGM 230K) is heading to North Motherwell with the steel plant in the background. The closure led to a loss of 770 jobs with another 10,000 jobs directly and indirectly affected.

D8 (TYS 261W) was a Dennis Dominator DD137B/Alexander RL-type H45/34F purchased new in June 1981, shown emerging from Anderston bus station in Glasgow. It was carrying a broadside advert for Laing Homes, who can trace their roots back to 1848, but its house building arm was sold to George Wimpey in 2002.

T297 (WSU 439S) was a 1977 Leyland Leopard/Alexander B53F disguised with an advert for Wellhall Garage in Hamilton who were Lada dealers. Lada made its name in Western Europe selling large volumes of the Fiat 124-based VAZ-2101, and its many derivatives, as an economy car during the 1980s. However, it was seen as downmarket and inspired many jokes such as 'What's the difference between a Lada and a golf ball? You can drive a golf ball 200 yards.'

GTD 483 was a Leyland Titan PD1/Alexander H30/26R purchased new by Accrington Corporation as their fleet number 103 in 1946. The bodywork was to Leyland design, but was built under subcontract. The bus was purchased by John Laurie of Hamilton t/a Chieftain in May 1959, and came to Central with the business in October 1961, and gave a couple of years of service before being dismantled for spares. Laurie's depot was located at High Blantyre Road, Burnbank, and continued in use until 1962.

T360 (GSU 842T) was a Leyland Leopard PSU3C/3R/Alexander B53F purchased new in April 1979, shown carrying an advert for the *Maid of the Loch*. The ship was operated in landlocked Loch Lomond and had to be built in situ. It was on the books of the Scottish Transport Group and in a last-ditch effort to drum up business, a few of the Group's buses were given this advert.

SP34 (JFS 978X) was a Seddon Pennine VII/Alexander Y-type B53F acquired with the Clarkston depot of Eastern Scottish in June 1985. It is shown fully repainted in Central Scottish livery and looking very smart. The use of advertising on the side panels of single-deckers became more widespread around this time.

GSX 888T was an Alexander T-type bodied Seddon Pennine VII seen in Airdrie while still carrying Eastern Scottish fleet names, although the Central fleet number SP11 has been added to the front. Central would build up a very mixed fleet of thirty-four Seddon Pennines.

AH25 (LHS 749V) was a Volvo Ailsa B55-10/Alexander AV-type H44/35F purchased new in November 1979, and shown with an advert for Landmark Furniture Warehouses. The chassis was fitted with the Volvo TD70 engine, a compact turbo-charged unit of 6.7 litres. The rest of the design was relatively simple, with beam axles and leaf springs. A Self-Changing Gears semi-automatic gearbox was used. The chassis was manufactured in Scotland by Ailsa, Volvo's British subsidiary in which it owned 75 per cent from 1974 until 1985.

YSG 651W was a Seddon Pennine VII/Alexander B53F purchased new by Eastern Scottish as their number S651 in December 1980. It is shown when still in Eastern green, but with a Central fleet name and number applied. The side advert was for the Airdrie Savings Bank, which is the only remaining independent savings bank in the UK.

T367 (GSU 849T) carries a very early example of Adbus vinyl advertising. In this case it was for British potatoes. The use of vinyl is widespread nowadays and it is truly amazing what can be printed on it, especially when combined with contravision that can be placed over the windows and still allow passengers to see out.

D47 (MNS 47Y) was a Dennis Dominator/Alexander RL-type H79F purchased new in March 1983. It was intended to be sold mainly with the Gardner 6LXB engine coupled up to a Voith DIWA transmission and a drop-centre rear axle, but a hub-reduction rear axle and other engine options including the Rolls-Royce Eagle, the Cummins L10, the turbocharged Gardner 6LXCT and DAF engines were also available.

SP27 (SSX 601V) is seen here on hire to Stevenson's of Uttoxeter, who were keen to snap up Seddon Pennine's cheaply as they found them very economical to run. This Seddon had been new to Eastern Scottish and was transferred to Central with Clarkston depot. As there were fewer Seddon's in the fleet it made sense to dispose of them and standardise on the more numerous Leyland Leopards when disposals were made after the disastrous strikes.

D37 (FGE 437X) was snapped in East Kilbride working on the 201 service to Hamilton. This service is probably the busiest route within Lanarkshire and is still run today by Firstbus, but extended through to Airdrie and has recently seen heavy investment in new buses. East Kilbride depot was once one of the most profitable in the Bus Group, and Hutchison's of Overtown were interested in taking it over at one time.

The delivery of ten coach-seated Leyland Olympians in 1986 were probably the most successful double-deckers Central had purchased for many years, and really looked the part with their modern interpretation of the livery. LO6 (C806 KHS) demonstrates this as it leaves Glasgow for East Kilbride on service 78, and note that there was no mention of the Redline name at this stage.

The size of the fleet names applied was looked at, and some buses received this larger style. T333 (EGB 65T) was running through Hamilton on a local service and shows the effect. It was quite effective, but after two crippling strikes the brand name became toxic and the company tried to distance itself with new names and liveries.

C42 (WGM 42K) carries the two-tone blue used by the coach fleet from 1955 to 1977. Although intended mainly for private hire, they were often used on longer-distance routes and C42 was working on service 71 bound for East Kilbride. The Bus Group often used paper stickers on the windscreens instead of proper destination blinds, but these were very difficult to read as a bus approached.

BL274 (EGM 274C) was a Bristol Lodekka FLF6G/ECW H78F purchased new in 1965. It was given a broadside advert for Ian Skelly Cars. Ian established his first VW–Audi outlet from a previously derelict site in Dalmarnock Road, Rutherglen, in 1974 and built up Europe's highest-volume VW–Audi chain before selling it to the Appleyard Group for £18.3 million in 1989. The bus was later used by Duncan Stewart Coaches of Dalmuir.

CS3 (NGM 863M) was a 7-foot-6-inches-wide Bedford VAS5/Duple Vista 25 C27F delivered new in November 1973 for use in East Kilbride. The Bedfords were supplied to the company by SMT (dealer) Glasgow, and tended to be replaced at regular intervals. CS3 ran for seven years before sale to James King of Kirkcowan.

AH7 (BGG 257S) was part of an order diverted from Alexanders (Fife) before delivery. Ten of these Volvo Ailsa B55-10/Alexander AV-type H79F double-deckers arrived in 1978 and looked superb in the traditional Central colours, complete with blank advert panels. Central became the largest SBG subsidiary in 1986 with a fleet of 470 vehicles operating from five depots.

There is nothing quite like the sight of a brand new bus. Bristol Lodekka FS6G B191 (AGM 691B) was awaiting collection from the Eastern Coachworks factory in Lowestoft in April 1964. ECW was nationalised in 1947 and for the next eighteen years, its business consisted mainly of building bus bodies, which were mounted on Bristol chassis, for state-owned bus operators. In 1965 a 25 per cent share was sold to Leyland Motors, which enabled ECW to sell to the private sector once again.

The Mark 2 Leyland Nationals were delivered in an all-over maroon colour, and N25 (MDS 858V) was given this experimental livery. It wasn't deemed a success and remained a one-off. The bus led a nomadic life, becoming Kelvin Scottish (1234), Western Scottish (778) and Ribble (907) in its lifetime.

Perth provides the backdrop for C14 as it heads for Aberdeen on Scottish Citylink service 965. C114 JCS was a Leyland Tiger TRCLXC/2RH/Duple 320 C49Ft purchased new in April 1986. It became Kelvin Central Buses number 4283 in 1989, and moved to Strathtay Scottish the following year, where it was re-registered to WLT 610.

Central were still specifying manual gearboxes in 1979, long after most other companies had moved on to semi-automatics. EGB 70T was a Leyland Leopard PSU3C/3R fitted with Alexander Y-type B53F bodywork. T338 remained into the KCB years, before disposal to Strathtay, where it was used both as a school bus and driver trainer.

The company caused a great surprise when an order for twenty Leopards was replaced by one for Nationals, purchased to ensure an early delivery. EGB 82T was a Leyland National 11351A/1R B52F delivered in December 1978 as fleet number N5. It passed to Western Scottish in 1989 and became their L580.

The company was so pleased with the livery on the Leyland Nationals that they tried to emulate it on other types. Sadly it did not weather too well and was abandoned after a few buses were trialled. T306 (WSU 448S) demonstrates the effect at Broomielaw in Glasgow. It was a Leyland Leopard PSU3C/4R/Alexander Y-type B53F purchased new in November 1977. It passed to Kelvin Central Buses (1448) in 1989 and was given a full repaint before sale to Loch Lomond Coaches a week later. On disposal it passed to Marbill of Beith for further service.

T437 (LUS 437Y) was one of the final batch of Leopards delivered in January 1983. It was a PSU3G/4R model fitted with Alexander Y-type B53F bodywork, which still looked good, and was captured in Wishaw. It would become Kelvin Central Buses number 1567, and would last into Firstbus days.

Central SMT hired one of its Dennis Dominators to Eastern Scottish in April 1985 giving it an overall advertisement for the Airdrie Savings Bank. It remained on hire to Eastern Scottish until Central took over Clarkston depot in June of that year. The reason was that Central did not wish to acquire any other types of deckers from the Eastern Fleet. D45 (MNS 45Y) was a Dennis Dominator DD162/Alexander RL-type H45/34F new in March 1983.

EGB 77T was a Dennis Dominator DD110/Alexander H74F purchased new by Central Scottish as their D1 in October 1978. It was one of two built (the other went to NBC subsidiary PMT) and the bodywork was a mixture of Alexander D type (as supplied on Fleetlines) married to some AV-type components. By the time of this shot it had also received an Ailsa-type front grill. It would later pass to Kelvin Central Buses in 1989 and receive fleet number 1701.

LT19 (OUS 19Y) was a Leyland Tiger TRBTL11/2R/Alexander TS-type B53F purchased new by Central Scottish in July 1983. The batch was delivered in this simple version of the livery, but was soon changed to the less practical zigzag version. LT19 was heading up North Hanover Street to Buchanan bus station in Glasgow.

B204 (AGM 704B) was a Bristol Lodekka FS6G/ECW H33/27RD purchased new in June 1964. It was snapped at the old Buchanan bus station in Glasgow. The waste ground used for parking vehicles was the site of the old Buchanan railway station, which closed in 1966. This bus station was mainly used by the Central, Eastern and Midland companies.

L484 (GM 6384) was an all Leyland Titan PD2/10 L27/28R purchased new by Central SMT in October 1954. The bus was withdrawn in 1969 and passed to Tiger Coaches (dealer), but was thankfully saved for preservation and has been restored to a very high standard. This view shows it at the premises of the now-defunct operator Irvine's of Law, where the bus was receiving mechanical attention.

KRG 515F was a Leyland Leopard PSU3/3R/Alexander Y-type B53F new to Alexander (Northern) in June 1968 as NPE15. As part of a deal to give more double-deckers to Northern it was transferred to Western SMT in January 1976 in exchange for Albion Lowlanders. It moved on again in 1981 to Central, who had a vehicle shortage at that time, and it is seen in Glasgow in that year.

LT36 (A36 VDS) was a Leyland Tiger TRBLXB/2RH/Alexander TS-type B53F delivered new in June 1984. It passed to Kelvin Central in 1989 and into Firstbus ownership when the business of SBL Holdings was acquired, and was later transferred to Lowland. It was caught in Hamilton with an overall advert for Trust Motors, who were Ford Dealers, owned by the Barr & Wallace Arnold Trust, who at the time also had a coach fleet.

AH8 (BGG 258S) was a Volvo Ailsa B55-10/Alexander AV-type H44/35F purchased in June 1978. The bus saw heavy use on the busy routes between Glagow and East Kilbride via Burnside and Rutherglen. On disposal in 1988 it passed to Eastern Scottish as their VV48 and lasted into SMT days. It was captured in Glasgow's Killermont Street bus station. As can be seen AH8 carries a broadside advert for The Ian Skelly Group. Ian is a former director of Rangers Football Club, but resigned from the post in 2003, with Rangers' debt estimated by some to be £80 million at that time.

A206 UYS was a Dennis Dorchester SDA806/Alexander TC-type C47F new to Central Scottish as their C6 in July 1984. It passed to Kelvin Central Buses (2186) and came into Firstbus ownership when Strathclyde Buses were acquired. However, all that was a long way in the future when it was still quite new and working for Scottish Citylink. It is shown arriving in Ayr bus station.

UGM 214K was a Leyland Leopard PSU3/3R/Alexander Y-type B53F purchased new as T114 in October 1971, seen in Hamilton depot. Traditionally Central used Lanarkshire registration marks with the letters VD, but this was changed to GM around 1953 when the boundaries of Motherwell were extended and included the company headquarters at Traction House.

EGB 78T was a Leyland National 11351A/1R B52F purchased new in December 1978 as fleet number N1. It became Western Scottish L578 in 1989, before joining Chase Bus Services for further service in the West Midlands. Note the in-house advert for the Lanarkshire to Blackpool express service operated during the summer months.

DD4 (A104 RGE) was captured at Old Kilpatrick working on service 134 to Drumchapel. It was a Dennis Dorchester SDA804/Alexander TS-type B53F purchased new in October 1983, at a time when Leyland refused to sell their Tiger models fitted with Gardner engines. This protest purchase forced Leyland to relent and later offer Gardner engines as an option.

The second batch of Leyland Nationals were delivered in all-over red, and quickly pressed into service with just a cream rectangle applied to take the fleet names. The fleet names were applied in blue after the SBG decided on a corporate style from 1978, with all subsidiaries included. N32 (MDS 865V) was new in April 1980, and would later pass to Kelvin Scottish in 1986 and Western Scottish in 1988.

The quest for more suitable buses for the East Kilbride local services continued, and the company decided to try the Ford AO609 fitted with Alexander (Belfast) bodywork. Two new buses were ordered and joined by a former demonstrator. Last in the batch, FS3 (SUS 265W) was picking up passengers in the town centre.

LHS 740V was a Volvo Ailsa B55-10/Alexander AV-type H79F purchased new in November 1979, shown at Alexander's Coachbuilding factory in Falkirk awaiting delivery. This batch introduced a creamier version of the livery that looked superb, but sadly did not weather well, so eventually they were all repainted into the older version of the colours. It later became Kelvin Central Buses number 1960.

Central SMT was by far the most profitable company in the Scottish Bus Group. Industrial Lanarkshire provided very good bus operating territory. 1963 Bristol FSF6G/ECW H70F (FGM 164) was loading in Brandon Parade in Motherwell while working service 95 to Newhouse.

MNS 44Y was a Dennis Dominator DD162/Alexander RL-type H79F purchased new by Central Scottish as their D44 in March 1983. It is seen at the old East Kilbride depot with sister D43 sitting behind. It passed to Kelvin Central Buses as their number 1744 in 1989.

EGB 82T was a Leyland National 11351A/1R B52F purchased new by Central Scottish in December 1978, and is shown sitting on the forecourt of Wishaw Depot. It passed to Western Scottish in 1989 and became their L580. Wishaw depot was closed by successor Kelvin Central Buses in December 1990.

CAG 449C was a Leyland Leopard PSU3/3R/Alexander Y-type C49F new as Western SMT L2034 in 1965. It was purchased by Central in 1981 to cover late delivery of new buses, becoming T407 briefly. The Western livery was kept but adapted to take Central Scottish fleet names, as shown in this view taken in East Kilbride.

WSU 430S was a Leyland Leopard PSU3C/3R/Alexander Y-type B53F purchased new by Central SMT as their T288 in September 1977. It passed to Kelvin Central as their 1430 in 1989, and went to Clydeside 2000 in 1994 (originally 620 but later renumbered to 459). That was all still a long way in the future when this picture was taken however. Central were experimenting with their livery at this time and consideration was given to make the Y types look more like the Nationals and T types. Only a few were done, and personally I rather liked it. Central management didn't approve it and all the buses were swiftly repainted back to the normal layout.

BL305 (FGM 305D) is seen on its holidays! It was on loan to sister company Alexander's (Fife) and was sitting by the sea at Kirkcaldy Esplanade, indeed a long way from industrial Lanarkshire. The Central SMT livery was passable in the area, where the buses ran in a brighter shade of red, and in the past ex-Central buses had been purchased and run in their old colours.

Newly delivered LT15 (OUS 15Y) was leaving Glasgow on the busy 62 service to Hamilton in its original livery, which looked really smart. It was a 1983 bus on a Leyland Tiger TRBTL11/2R chassis, which had been introduced to replace the Leopard. Alexander fitted their TS Style body, which was designed for Central and based on the TE and TC designs then going into production.

EGB 81T was a Leyland National 11351A/1R B52F purchased new by Central Scottish as their N4 in December 1978, and photographed in Wishaw town centre. On the formation of Kelvin Central Buses in 1989 it was deemed surplus and passed to Western Scottish as their fleet number AL581 before sale to Choice Travel in the Midlands.

HGM 443E was a Leyland Leopard PSU3/1R/Alexander Y-type B53F purchased new by Central SMT as their T43 in 1967. It still looked smart eleven years later as it left Glasgow on service 55 to Netherburn. The company had yet to introduce the straight waistband on their buses, making T43 look quite old.

C261 FGG was a Leyland Tiger TRCLX/2RH/Alexander TE-type C49F purchased new in September 1985. It leads a streak of Tigers out of Buchanan bus station during the evening peak. LT61 would later join Kelvin Central Buses where it became number 2279. It was quickly sold to Strathtay Scottish where it became number ST22 with registration number HSK 792.

A29 VDS was a Leyland Tiger TRBLXB/2R/Alexander TS-type B53F new to the company in June 1984. It was photographed during peak hour coming into Glasgow's Buchanan bus station with the destination screen already set for the return leg. This livery was eye-catching, but not really practical for service buses as there were too many colour breaks in the panels and any replacement panels needed a lot of work in masking for the paint to match.

Leyland National N1 (EGB 78T) expresses a wish to return to its home depot of Wishaw as it waits for the traffic lights to change at the exit from Anderston bus station in Glasgow. It was one of a handful to enter service in the mainly maroon version of the livery, which I have to admit rather appealed to me. None lasted very long before they were brought in to line with the creamier version applied to the rest of the batch.

BE219 (CGM 719C) was at the same place a few years earlier, working on a journey to West Crindledyke on service 64. The ECW bodywork on this Bristol Lodekka shows the neat way the livery was cleaned up to accommodate the blue corporate fleet names adopted in 1978. The Western Scottish bus in the background shows how the different shades used allowed passengers to identify their bus.

Leyland Tiger/Alexander TS-type B53F B258 BYS was on order by Central Scottish at the time Kelvin Scottish was created in June 1985 and delivered new to that firm in June 1986 as their fleet number T147. Kelvin had assumed responsibility for Central's services in Dunbartonshire. It was originally intended to be Central fleet number LT58, matching the registration number. It was swapped for a Leyland National and given the next vacant Central fleet number which was LT63, as the number LT58 had been reused by Central for C258 FGG.

C16 (D316 SGB) was a smart Leyland Tiger TRCTL11/3RZ/Duple 340 C49Ft purchased new in May 1987 for Scottish Citylink work. It passed to Kelvin Central Buses as their number 4306 in 1989, but was resold to Strathtay Scottish after Citylink work was abandoned as unprofitable. It became number ST26, and later 426 with Strathtay, eventually being re-registered as 365 DXU, it was finally D841 COS before disposal in 2001.

LT2 (FGG 602X) was a Leyland Tiger TRBTL11/2R/Alexander T-type C49F purchased new by Central Scottish in May 1982, and at a glance looked very similar to the dual-purpose Leopards already in the fleet. It was caught in Hamilton, loading for a journey to Airdrie. It would last into Kelvin Central days as number 2202.

RFS 586V was a Leyland National NL116L11/1R B52F purchased new by Eastern Scottish in April 1980 as their fleet number N586. It came into Central ownership with Clarkston depot in June 1986, and was snapped at Coatbridge bus stance. It was still in Eastern green, but with Central fleet names complete with 'Best Bus' logos. It would become Kelvin Scottish 1226 within a year.

AH19 (LHS 743V) was a Volvo Ailsa B55-10/Alexander AV-type H44/35F bought new in 1979. The broadside advert for Barratt was quite common at the time with buses throughout the country carrying it. Barratt Developments PLC is one of the largest residential property development companies in the United Kingdom, and was founded in 1958 as Greensitt Bros, but control was later assumed by Sir Lawrie Barratt.

1986 Leyland Olympian ONLXB/1RH/Alexander R-type CH47/27F LO10 (C810 KHS) leaves Glasgow with a good load on Redline service X3 bound for East Kilbride Greenhills. These Limited Stop commuter services were very popular with passengers. Successor company KCB moved the batch to Airdrie when East Kilbride depot closed.

T381 (GSU 863T) was a Leyland Leopard PSU3C/3R fitted with Alexander Y-type B53F bodywork, which had been built at their Belfast factory in July 1979. Walter Alexander Coachbuilders was a builder of bus and coach bodywork based in Falkirk. The company was formed in 1947 to continue the coachbuilding activities of W. Alexander & Sons after their bus service operation was nationalised. After several mergers and changes of ownership it now forms part of Alexander Dennis.

T371 (GSU 853T) was a Leyland Leopard PSU3C/3R/Alexander T-type C49F purchased new in April 1979. Coaches had carried a two-tone blue colour scheme between 1955 and 1977, but this was changed when heavyweight chassis were specified later. This allowed greater use on stage carriage services if required, as well as coachwork.

B81 (GM 9281) was a Bristol Lodekka LD6G/ECW H33/27R purchased new in 1958. The point of its design and introduction was to end the uncomfortable and inconvenient low-bridge double-deck bus layout, replacing it by lowering the chassis frame and integrating it with the body, and fitting a drop-centre rear axle, so that there were no steps from the rear entrance platform to the front of the passenger gangway.

Dennis Dominator DD137B/Alexander RL-type H78F D38 (FGE 438X) is disguised by an overall advert for Thermaglaze replacement windows. It was turning out of Osborne Street in Glasgow, heading for Faifley. This area is now occupied by the St Enoch shopping centre, construction of which began in 1986 with completion three years later.

The Glasgow Garden Festival was held in the city between April and September 1988, and attracted 4.3 million visitors over 152 days. Many of the visitors arrived by bus and coach, and a dedicated coach park was opened on the site of the former Ibrox bus garage. Central had its fair share of hires and LT1 (FGG 601X) was on duty on one of these. It was a Leyland Tiger TRBTL11/2R fitted with Alexander T-type C49F coachwork.

T149 (XGM 449L) was a Leyland Leopard PSU3/3R/Alexander Y-type B53F new to the company in September 1972. It was caught in Osborne Street in Glasgow on a journey to Cathkin on route 72. The 'Best Bus Around' decals on the side are possibly controversial, and over optimistic, but that did not stop Tyne and Wear Omnibus purchasing it for further service.

The Asda name first saw light of day 1965 with the merger of the Asquith chain of supermarkets and Associated Dairies, and indeed Asda is an abbreviation of Asquith and Dairies. Central's Dennis Dominator D35 (FGE 435X) was promoting the supermarket chain as it passed through Glasgow on its way to Anderston bus station.

Leyland Tiger TRBTL11/2R/Alexander TS-type B53F LT17 (OUS 17Y) was new in July 1983 and shows the original livery applied to the type as it heads for Newmains on service 60. Fleet numbers for the Tiger class would reach up to LT83 in due course.

LSC 934T was a Seddon Pennine VII/Alexander Y-type B53F purchased new by Eastern Scottish as their number S934 in June 1979. It is seen with Central when still in Eastern livery, but with its new fleet names and numbers applied, as it arrives in Glasgow. The area behind the bus is now the site of the Buchanan Galleries shopping centre.

A vehicle shortage was averted by the hiring in of buses from other Group members, including Northern and Western Scottish. PRS 120J was a Leyland Leopard PSU3/3R/Alexander Y-type B53F new as Alexander (Northern) NPE20 in February 1971, while a semi-automatic Western Leopard is seen in the background. It was said that the company received letters from passengers saying how much better the service was now that Western were running it!

The bodywork on T331 (EGB 63T) was built at the Belfast factory of Alexander Coachbuilders in February 1979. In 1969 the company bought out Potters, a bodybuilder in Northern Ireland, and set up a subsidiary Walter Alexander & Co (Belfast) Limited. The ownership of the company subsequently changed several times. In 1990 the family sold the company to Spotlaunch plc., but within two years a management buyout occurred and it became a standalone company until 1995, when it was bought by the Mayflower Corporation plc. In 2001 it was incorporated into TransBus International and is now part of Alexander Dennis.

D48 (MNS 48Y) was a Dennis Dominator DD162 fitted with Alexander RL-type H45/34F bodywork and dated from March 1983. It received a broadside advert with promotional material for three different businesses: The Savoy Centre in Glasgow, Clydebank Shopping Centre and The Plaza Shopping Centre in East Kilbride.

VMS 108J was obtained from Alexander (Midland) in 1975 in exchange for the ill-fated Daimler Fleetlines. It was a Leyland Leopard PSU3/3R/Alexander Y-type B53F built in January 1971 as Midland MPE108, and was passing through Wishaw Cross on service 240 when snapped. The 240 service to Glasgow ran from Lanark and passed through many towns in industrial Lanarkshire.

EGB 92T was a Leyland National 11351A/1R B52F new as Central SMT N15 in January 1979. The Leyland National was a single-deck bus manufactured in large quantities between 1972 and 1985. It was developed as a joint project between two UK state-owned companies – the National Bus Company and British Leyland. Buses were constructed at a specially built factory at the Lillyhall Industrial Estate, Workington. Styling was carried out by the famed Italian vehicle stylist Giovanni Michelotti.

T319 (EGB 51T) heads along Argyle Street to Anderston bus station with the destination already set for the return journey. I must admit Bonkle is one of my favourite places listed on a destination screen. The Y type was a long-running design built by Walter Alexander Coachbuilders of Falkirk, built on a wide range of chassis between 1962 and 1983.

AH25 (LHS 749V) was an example of an all-Scottish product, with the chassis built in Irvine and the bodywork in Falkirk. In 1977, an improved Mark II version of the Volvo Ailsa appeared, with two transmission options offered, a Self-Changing Gears pneumo-cyclic unit or a Voith D851 with retarder. A higher driving position featured, and was noticeable on the cream above the cab being out of line.

PGA 829V was a Leyland Leopard PSU3F/4R/Alexander T-type C49F purchased new in June 1980 as T389, seen in Anderston bus station in Glasgow. It passed to Kelvin Scottish (2051) in June 1985 and on to Western Scottish (L499) in 1988, where it was refurbished. It joined Shuttle Buses in 1994 and was re-registered as DAZ 8290.

TSU 643W was a Leyland Leopard PSU3G/4R/Alexander Y-type B53F new as T420 in March 1981, advertising The Airdrie Savings Bank, which is a small commercial bank operation with eight branches in Lanarkshire. In August 2010 it received a cash injection of £10 million from a group of Scottish entrepreneurs. Sir Angus Grossart, Sir David Murray, Ann Gloag, Brian Souter, Sir Tom Farmer and Ewan Brown each provided £1 million.

Advertising seemed to be taking more and more space on the side panels, as shown by T431 (LUS 431Y) at Anderston bus station in Glasgow. This Leopard/Y type was new in January 1983, and among the final batch to be purchased as Leyland were discontinuing the model in favour of the Leyland Tiger.

A205 UYS was a Dennis Dorchester SDA806/Alexander TC-type C47F new as C5 in July 1984 in coach livery. It was renumbered to DD14 and given the zigzag style of colours when captured in Hamilton while working on Scottish Citylink service 982 bound for the Scottish capital.

The Glasgow Garden Festival held in 1988 provided lots of hires for Central, and two Leyland Olympians were present when snapped together. LO9/10 (C809/10KHS) were new in 1986 and took the Bus Group into more modern vehicle policies, with the use of large destination displays and coach seating, coupled with a modern twist on the traditional livery.

June 1985 saw the biggest shake-up of the Scottish Bus Group since the Alexander Empire was split into three companies in 1961. The bus-operating subsidiaries were increased from seven to eleven companies, more geographically based to match council boundaries. This ensured that each council only had to deal with one SBG company in each area and this simplified the subsidies. SP26 had just been transferred from Eastern Scottish and had yet to be repainted.

LT9 (MNS 9Y) was loading in St Andrews Square bus station in Edinburgh for the return journey to East Kilbride. Scottish Citylink was also set up as a stand-alone operation in June 1985 to coordinate express services throughout Scotland and beyond. The use of a single brand brought most express services together and emphasised a single network.

Alaska Jacks frozen food shop in Motherwell were promising 'The bearest prices in town' on T354 (GSU 836T) as it left Anderston bus station in Glasgow. This Leyland Leopard PSU3C/3R/Alexander Y-type B53F was new in April 1979, and was already outmoded when new, with high floor, narrow entrance and manual gearbox.

T386 (PGA 826V) was a 1980 Leyland Leopard PSU3F/4R fitted with Alexander T-type C49F coachwork. It was repainted into the zigzag livery and is shown resting in East Kilbride bus station. Demolition work on the derelict Stuart Hotel took place in 2009 after being served with an urgent demolition order by South Lanarkshire Council. The crumbling structure had decayed to such a parlous state that emergency action had to be taken.

Central operated thirty Ailsas bought in two batches in 1978 and 1979. The Scottish Bus Group had considerable influence over the development of this vehicle in a bid to return to the relative simplicity of a front-engined design. The Ailsa combined this with the need to allow one-man operation, by squeezing a small turbocharged Volvo engine onto the front overhang. AH18 was bound for Strathaven.

T304 (WSU 446S) wears the pre-corporate style used up until 1978, when all SBG companies were forced to use a standard style of blue fleet name coupled with a saltire flag. Companies could still specify their own liveries, although some had to be altered to allow the blue fleet names to be accommodated.

Alexander R-type bodied Dennis Dominator D33 (FGE 433X) carried an all-over advert for Berger paint. The firm began in 1760 when Louis Amelius Christanus Adolphus Steigenberger came to England from Frankfurt and by 1770 shortened his name to Lewis Berger. He was manufacturing pigments in East London, initially in Limehouse.

A busy scene in Coliseum coach station in Blackpool shows a pair of Central T-type Leopards working on service 987, which was a summer-only Saturday express service from Lanarkshire to Lancashire. PGA 831V on the left was a PSU3F/4R model with fully automatic transmission and carried fleet number T391, while GSU 853T was a PSU3C/3R model with 4-speed manual gearbox.

SSX 598V was a Seddon Pennine VII/Alexander Y-type B53F purchased new by Eastern Scottish in February 1980 as their fleet number S598. It is shown fully repainted by Central Scottish. It was based at Clarkston garage and was heading for Caldercruix on service 257.

LT21 (A21 VDS) was a Leyland Tiger TRBLXB/2RH/Alexander TS-type B53F purchased new by Central Scottish in May 1984. The Tiger was launched in 1981 and initially only one engine was offered, the turbocharged Leyland TL11. Leyland had lost SBG orders to Seddon's Pennine 7, owing to their unwillingness to offer a Gardner engine. When they launched the Tiger, it continued this same approach just as Dennis was developing the Gardner-engined Dennis Dorchester, which similarly had the potential to win Scottish Bus Group orders away from the Tiger.

OGM 282H was a Leyland Leopard PSU3/1R /Alexander Y-type B53F new to Central SMT in 1970. It is seen at Motherwell Depot carrying the post-1978 corporate fleet names and still looks very smart. Note the pay-as-you-enter notices applied.

The Dodge 50 Series, later known as the Renault 50 Series, were light commercial vehicles produced in the UK by Dodge and later Renault between 1979 and 1993. They were popular with SBG as automatic gearboxes were fitted. In 1994 Renault sold the production tooling to a Chinese manufacturer. The 50 series is still being produced in China under a different name. Central's R9 was an exhibit on the Alexander stand at the 1987 Motor Show.

The 1985 Scottish Bus Group reorganisation saw the transfer of the Eastern Scottish Airdrie depot to Central Scottish bringing with it a fleet of thirty-three Seddons, a rare type for the Central fleet as they only had one from Western SMT specially adapted for wheelchair access. SP2 (KSX 689N) was the oldest one inherited and is seen in Coatbridge working on service 245 bound for Muirhead.

D16 (TGM 216J) was a member of the ill-fated batch of Daimler Fleetline CRG6LXB/ECW H43/34F delivered new in 1971. These buses were numbered D1–35 and featured Gardner engines. However, for whatever reason the batch only lasted around three years. By the summer of 1974 rumours were circulating that Bristol Omnibus was going to buy them, but in the event other SBG companies took them. In hindsight it was the wrong move to make as they enjoyed full lives elsewhere.

Central bought very few single-deckers before 1961, when a batch of six short Leyland Leopards arrived. The batch was numbered as T1–6, before being reclassified as TS1–6 in 1965. They spent most of their lives at Carluke, Wishaw and Hamilton depots, often seeing service on Limited Stop services from Biggar and Peebles into Glasgow.

1979 saw the company begin to move with the times, using passenger friendly Leyland Nationals. This aerial view taken in Anderston bus station in Glasgow shows a cross-section of the fleet at the time. Semi-automatic gearboxes were specified for the following years' orders long after the industry had accepted them as the norm.

Former Eastern Scottish Seddon Pennine VII/Alexander Y-type B53F SP5 (CFS 827S) received a version of the zigzag livery and was easily spotted in the Central fleet on account of its long bay windows. The Seddons were withdrawn en masse by successor company Kelvin Central Buses as they were deemed non-standard.

Yet another version of the livery was applied on Nationals later in their lives. N23 (MDS 856V) demonstrates the point as it emerges from Anderston bus station in Glasgow, bound for Newmains. It had been new to the company in April 1980, and lasted into Kelvin Central days as their number 1132. It would see further service as First Provincial 404 in 1996.

It has been said that Eastern Scottish only agreed to take the National to enable an agreement on a one-man operation to take place at the former Baxters Victoria depot in Airdrie. Apparently once agreed, management only had three months to enact it or it would all have to be renegotiated. A stock batch of Leyland National 11351A/1R B52F were quickly delivered, including BSF 770S. It would pass to Central with the Airdrie routes in 1985, and was caught in Glasgow still wearing its former owner's livery.

T386 (PGA 826V) was a Leyland Leopard PSU3F/4R fitted with Alexander T-type C49F coachwork and was new in June 1980. It was repainted into the zigzag livery when captured in Glasgow while working on service 70 which connected Glasgow–Rutherglen–Burnside–Cathkin–East Kilbride–Strathaven.

When Central adopted a creamier version of its livery it did not weather well, and soon looked unkempt as exemplified by Volvo Ailsa AH17 (LHS 741V). This was also working on route 70, bound for Strathaven. I can remember one spirited ride on this service in particular, hanging on for dear life as we sped through Glasgow and beyond.

Leyland Leopard T160 (XGM 460L) also received the creamier livery, which looked quite modern with the beading simplified in this view taken in Helensburgh, which was the western-most extremity in the Central route network. It was heading for the Glasgow housing scheme of Drumchapel via Clydebank. Drumchapel was annexed from Dunbartonshire in 1938 as part of the overspill policy of Glasgow Corporation. A huge housing estate was built here in the 1950s to house 34,000 people and services were provided by both the corporation and Scottish Bus Group.

D22 (FGE 422X) was a Dennis Dominator DD137B/Alexander RL-type H45/34F purchased new by Central in June 1982. It later became Kelvin Scottish 1560 and Kelvin Central Buses 1722. The Central numbering scheme was based on letter prefixes indicating vehicle type, was adopted in 1932 and survived right until the end.

A peek inside Hamilton depot shows Ford A series BUS 347S alongside Leopard OGM 614M. At one time Hamilton boasted two depots, with premises at Burnbank Road, acquired from J. W. & R. Torrance in 1932, and at Bothwell Road, which had been the main garage of Glasgow Omnibus Company (G. O. C.). Burnbank Road closed in 1962 and Bothwell Road in 1988.

MDS 867V was a Leyland National NL116L11/1R B52F purchased new in April 1980 as fleet number N34. It was captured in Motherwell town centre. Note the advert for the Blackpool service which ran every Saturday from 2 June until 29 September and cost £11.50 for a single.

PGM 247M was a Bedford YRQ/Duple Dominant C45F purchased new as C47 in May 1974. It was sold to Tiger Coaches (dealer) in March 1977 before passing to Georgeson and Moore of Scalloway, Johnson of Brae, and Bolt's of Lerwick.

B153 (DGM 453) was a Bristol Lodekka FSF6G/ECW H34/26F delivered new in April 1962, seen in Churchill Avenue in East Kilbride. It would go for scrap to Trevor Wigley of Carlton (dealer) in April 1979. 218 examples of the FSF Series Bristol Lodekka were constructed and delivered to eleven Tilling Group operators during the period 1960–63.

C12 (C112 JCS) was a Leyland Tiger TRCLXC/2RH/Duple 320 C49Ft purchased new by Central Scottish in April 1986 for use on Scottish Citylink work. It would later serve with Kelvin Central Buses, Western Scottish, Clydeside 2000 and MacEwan's of Dumfries.

AGM 625B was a Leyland Leopard PSU3/3R/Alexander Y-type B53F purchased new in July 1964 as fleet number T25, shown in Churchill Avenue in East Kilbride. It entered service in January 1965 and was converted to OMO in 1971.

Faced with problems of high inflation and dwindling passenger numbers, the Midland Red Omnibus Company Limited commissioned their Viable Network Project in 1976 as a joint programme in conjunction with National Bus Company and independent consultants. The aim of the project was to identify passenger travel patterns and requirements. The project was later renamed as the Market Analysis Project or MAP. It was extended to Scotland as Scotmap and Central used this Bristol Lodekka to gather information.

Central's manual gearbox Leyland Leopards made good recovery vehicles for the fleet. Former T26 (HGM 426E) is seen ready for action in Motherwell depot. The neat conversion was carried out in June 1980.

Sister bus T27 (HGM 427E) was also converted to a recovery vehicle and shows the earlier livery carried. It was renumbered as S54 and was in a soggy Glasgow Buchanan bus station to coax a disabled bus back to life.

The rest of the book depicts the attempted rebranding of the fleet, which ultimately failed and led to the closure of the business. At the time everyone was optimistic and we all looked forward to following the fortunes of three companies instead of just one. LT62 (C262 FGG) was given Monklands Bus colours, based on the former independent Baxter's of Airdrie. This Alexander TE bodied Leyland Tiger passed to Strathtay Scottish in 1990 as their ST23 with the registration number WLT 784.

A bright red was adopted for Lanarkshire Bus as demonstrated by LT66 (B261 BYS). This Alexander TS-type B53F bodied Leyland Tiger was captured at Glasgow's Anderston bus station. This rebrand involved vehicles from Motherwell, Hamilton and Wishaw depots and brings back memories of the Lanarkshire Traction Company which was absorbed in November 1949.

The third identity was EK Chieftain for vehicles based at East Kilbride. This sought to bring back memories of the former Laurie Brothers operations which were taken over in 1962 and traded as Chieftain. The livery was not as old as people seemed to think and Chieftain had only adopted it in 1951. The original company used a fleet name which was made from raised metal letters screwed onto the buses. T400 (PUS 155W) was caught in Hamilton.

D373 OSU was a Leyland Tiger TRCLXB/2RH/Alexander TS-type B53F purchased new in January 1987 as Central Scottish LT73. The Monklands Bus livery looked superb and classy with the only reference to Central Scottish Omnibuses being the legal lettering carried on the side panels.

The EK Chieftain fleet also contained some double-deckers such as Volvo Ailsa B55-10/Alexander AV-type H79F LHS 749V, which had been purchased new in November 1979 as AH25. By a fluke the adverts on the side panels even matched the cream used in the livery. It was heading back to East Kilbride on service 77.

The Monklands Bus fleet also contained some Leyland Nationals such as GSX 867T. New as Eastern Scottish N867 in October 1978. It ironically led to the disappearance of the original Baxter's of Airdrie livery that the company was now trying to adopt. After the decision to close the company, the Nationals all went to Western Scottish, including examples removed from the paint shops in undercoat for the new livery.

FGE 435X was a Dennis Dominator DD137B/Alexander RL-type H45/33F purchased new by Central Scottish as their number D35 in July 1982. The Bus Group were multi-sourcing new vehicles from several manufacturers at the time. This East Kilbride-based bus received Chieftain livery, and was returning to East Kilbride on an X2 express working.

After the competitive services launched in Glasgow under the 'Harrier' brand failed to live up to expectations, the minibus fleet was rebranded as 'Little Chiefs and used on Hamilton local services, and R21 (D821 RYS) demonstrates the point. It was a Dodge S56/Alexander B21F purchased new by Central in May 1987.

The Monklands Bus identity really suited the lines of the Alexander Y-type B53F body fitted to this Leyland Leopard PSU3G/4R. It had been new in April 1981 as T425, and was captured in Buchanan bus station in Glasgow with the destination screen set for its home depot.

The Lanarkshire Bus identity would become the most widespread, with many buses receiving it. It would form the basis of the new merged KCB company livery with the fleet names altered to read Kelvin Central Buses in the same style. LT41 was heading for Strathaven on service 54.

LHS 744V was a Volvo Ailsa B55-10/Alexander AV-type H44/35F purchased new by Central Scottish as their AH20 in November 1979. It also received EK Chieftain colours and had just arrived in Glasgow. It must have been running late as the destination screen has already been set for its return journey.

Only one Leyland Leopard/Alexander Y type received Lanarkshire Bus colours. The former T399 (PUS 154W) was sitting on the forecourt of Wishaw depot a couple of weeks before the merger with Kelvin Scottish, but the fleet numbers had already been changed.

D373 OSU was a Leyland Tiger TRCLXB/2RH/Alexander TS-type B53F purchased new by Central Scottish as their LT73 in January 1987. We can only speculate about how the company could have achieved transfers of vehicles between garages without the need for a total repaint.